DUE DATE

MAY 24 1994			
MAR 11 1996			
DEC 20 1996			
MAY 08 1997			
FE 16 '00			
FE 29 '00			
MR 21 '00			
FE 26 '01			
MR 26 '01			
	201-6503		Printed in USA

Everything You Need to Know About
DISCRIMINATION

Prejudice against racial or cultural differences often separates people from each other.

• THE NEED TO KNOW LIBRARY •

Everything You Need to Know About

DISCRIMINATION

Ezra Palmer

Series Editor: Evan Stark, Ph.D.

THE ROSEN PUBLISHING GROUP, INC.
NEW YORK

Published in 1990, 1993 by The Rosen Publishing Group, Inc.
29 East 21st Street, New York, NY 10010

Revised Edition 1993
Copyright 1990, 1993 by The Rosen Publishing Group, Inc.

Manufactured in the United States of America.

Library of Congress Cataloging-in-Publication Data

Palmer, Ezra.
    Everything you need to know about discrimination / Ezra Palmer.
    (The Need to know library)
    Includes bibliographical references and index.
    ISBN 0-8239-1656-1
    Summary: Discusses prejudice in such areas as religion, race, nationality, sex, and physical disability and how it can lead to discrimination in jobs, housing, and general treatment in the modern world.
    1. Toleration—Juvenile literature. 2. Discrimination—Juvenile literature. [1. Prejudices. 2. Discrimination. 3. Toleration.]
  I. Title. II. Series.
HM276.P17   1990
303.3'85—dc20   90-36018
                                      CIP
                                        AC

Contents

Introduction

John won't let Nancy into his club because her skin is a different color. Louisa doesn't like Peter because of his religion. Lydia won't allow Claudia to play on her basketball team because Claudia speaks with an accent.

These are all examples of discrimination.

Discrimination means being less polite, less kind, even cruel to someone because she or he is different. The difference can be race or religion. It can be nationality or the color of a person's skin. The difference can even be a physical disability.

Many people have been hurt by discrimination. People have been denied jobs because of it. Others have been denied places to live. There are laws to protect people against actions that arise from discrimination.

Sometimes victims of discrimination only have their feelings hurt. Hurting a person's feelings isn't against the law, but it is wrong.

You meet new people every day. A new family moves into the building where you live. A new kid enters your homeroom class. Sometimes you like these new people right away. Someone new may enjoy the same sports that you do. Maybe he or she likes the same subjects in school, or has the same sense of humor that you do.

But suppose you don't like someone you meet? Is that discrimination? That depends on your reasons. Imagine you meet someone who likes hockey. Your favorite sport is baseball. The two of you don't have much in common. You decide not to pursue a friendship. That *isn't* discrimination. Your decision was based on your judgment of that person as an *individual*. You did not make your decision because of the person's race, religion, or color. You did not make your decision because the person was female. You did not dislike her because her grandparents were born in Japan.

We are all individuals. Each of us has likes and dislikes. We like some people better than we like others. That is okay. But discrimination—deciding not to like someone because of color, or religion, or race—is wrong.

The elderly are often discriminated against in our society.

Chapter 1

What Is Discrimination?

Discrimination begins with prejudice, the idea that one group is better than another. Members of one group might think that everyone belonging to another group is stupid, or ugly. They might believe that members of another group do not work as hard. They might think that the culture of another group is not as good as their group. Beliefs like these have existed all through history. Unfortunately, people still believe them today.

Most modern societies are made up of many kinds of people. In a society with many different groups there is always some discrimination. Almost always, the *majority* group discriminates against other groups. The majority is the largest, most powerful group in the society. Other groups are called *minorities*.

What happens if the majority discriminates against other groups? That depends. Sometimes the majority makes laws that are unfair to minority groups. The laws might deny a right such as voting.

In our society, there are many examples of discrimination. The first example most of us think of is racial discrimination.

About a hundred years ago, most African Americans in North America were slaves. Slavery was outlawed in the United States in the 1860s. New laws were passed then. Those laws limited the rights of African Americans. Those laws said where these minority citizens could live and work. Today, of course, slavery no longer exists. Laws have been passed to protect the rights of all minorities. But there is still discrimination against African Americans.

Slavery was one of the worst kinds of discrimination.

Leaders in the Fight Against Discrimination

Nelson Mandela

Usually the majority in a society makes rules that discriminate against the minority. In some societies, however, the majority does not always make the rules. In South Africa, for instance, there are nearly four blacks to every white. But through a system of rules called *apartheid*, whites control society.

Apartheid is a policy of strict racial *segregation* that discriminates against blacks and other groups, such as Indians and other Asians. Blacks cannot live in the same areas as whites. They do not have the same voting rights. They cannot hold the same kinds of jobs. The rules of apartheid keep whites in control.

Until recently, everything in South Africa was segregated. Segregation means separation of people of different races. Schools are separate. Homes are in separate areas. Stores are separate. Even hospitals treat either blacks or whites, but not both. There is still segregation in South Africa. But the country is gradually beginning to change. In February of 1990, *Nelson Mandela* was released from prison after 27 years. He is the leader of the ANC, the African National Congress. The ANC has called for equal rights for black South Africans, including the right to vote.

The President of South Africa, F.W. de Klerk, started holding talks with black organizations, including the ANC. In 1992, 69 percent of South African voters voted in favor of de Klerk's program for change. But talks between blacks and whites broke down because of violence against blacks. In 1993 the talks were resumed, but the change from the discrimination of apartheid will be slow and difficult.

That is only one example of discrimination in the United States. Asians, Native Americans, Latin Americans, and many others also face discrimination there. In other countries there are other minority groups. Canada was settled by French and English colonists. Today French Canadians are members of a minority. Australia was settled by the English, too. Now the native Australian people are minority citizens.

Women everywhere are members of another group that has to fight discrimination. Older citizens and people who are physically handicapped also face discrimination. Mentally retarded people face discrimination also.

Some discrimination is against the law. For example, an employer cannot deny a woman a job just because she is a woman. Students cannot be sent to a separate school because their skin is a different color. No family can be forbidden to buy a home anywhere because of who they are.

But some discrimination isn't illegal. You may decide that you don't like people whose skin or race or language is different than yours. That is prejudice. Having that feeling isn't against the law. The law can't change some people's feelings. But legal or illegal, prejudice and discrimination are wrong.

Chapter 2

Individual Rights

How did prejudice and discrimination begin? No one really knows. It is likely that as long as man has been on earth, discrimination has been on earth too. The Bible, for instance, tells the story of how the Jews were slaves in Egypt. Today, however, most discrimination is against the law.

How did that change happen? It began a long time ago, with the idea of *individual rights*. Individual rights include *civil rights*, such as the right to vote or run for political office. They also include *social rights*, such as the right to choose where to live and work.

About 700 years ago, there were no such rights for most people. That time in history is called the Middle Ages. Only the rich and powerful people in society had any rights. They were the "nobles." The majority of the people were either common freemen or serfs. Freemen had little power and few personal rights. Serfs had even fewer. Whatever rights the nobles, freemen and serfs had were not written down anywhere.

The first step in the fight for individual rights came in England in the year 1215. King John had become unpopular. Taxes were high. Sending men to fight in faraway lands was dangerous and expensive. Nobles and peasants were fighting for England in wars. The nobles had to supply everything. And they had to follow King John's orders no matter what the result. The nobles of England banded together. They thought the king was abusing his power. The nobles forced King John to sign the Magna Carta, or "great charter." It was a small step toward ending discrimination. But it was an important beginning.

The Magna Carta gave freemen the right to a trial by jury. But it didn't really help the average person. It released the nobles from many of King John's harsh laws. It allowed the nobles to elect people who would share some of the

The signing of The Declaration of Independence, July 4, 1776. It includes the idea that "all men are created equal."

power with the king. Those elections were the beginning of a new system of government.

From that beginning, the idea of equality began to grow. As the years passed, others in England were given the right to vote and to help make laws. Then, in 1689, England passed its Bill of Rights, which gave many rights to its citizens.

Less than a hundred years later the people of the United States of America were fighting for independence from England. The idea of equality was very important to the early Americans.

Leaders in the Fight Against Discrimination

Susan B. Anthony

Susan B. Anthony was born in 1820. After finishing her education she worked as a teacher, and then she managed the family farm.

Susan B. Anthony was opposed to slavery and worked to end it. She realized something very important. Some abolitionists, even though they were against slavery, discriminated against women. Anthony decided to work to end that discrimination.

Susan B. Anthony helped to found the American Equal Rights Association and the National Woman Suffrage Association. In 1872, she was arrested for trying to vote.

Her dream of winning the right to vote for women finally came true. But Susan B. Anthony did not live to see it. She died in 1906, fourteen years before the passage of the 19th Amendment. The amendment gave American women the right to vote.

In the Declaration of Independence, Thomas Jefferson wrote: "All men are created equal."

Jefferson was also one of the men who wrote the guiding rules for the United States, the Constitution. They also wrote the first ten additions, or "amendments," to the Constitution. These additions are called "The Bill of Rights."

Most people, once they get to know each other, find they have many things in common.

But even with the Declaration of Independence, the Constitution, and the Bill of Rights, citizens of the United States were not truly equal. Most blacks were slaves. The free blacks didn't have equal rights. Women, too, were discriminated against. They weren't allowed to vote. Under the law, the property of married women belonged to their husbands.

As the years passed, more and more people in the United States began to believe that slavery must end. These people were known as abolitionists. They wanted to abolish slavery. But the people in the southern states did not want the system to change. Their economy depended on slave workers.

When Abraham Lincoln was elected president of the United States, the southern states split away to make their own country. This was the beginning of the American Civil War. In 1863, in the middle of the war, Lincoln declared all slaves in the rebel states were free. This was called the Emancipation Proclamation. But the war was not over. The southern states followed their own rules. Slavery did not end until the North had won the war.

Slavery is one of the most terrible forms of discrimination. It deprives a person of his or her freedom, of all individual rights. In the United States slavery was based on race. Blacks were brought from Africa by slave

Mohandas K. Gandhi

Leaders in the Fight Against Discrimination

Mohandas K. Gandhi was born in India in 1869. He is known as one of the most famous fighters for individual rights. Gandhi developed a new way to fight discrimination. He did not believe in using violence.

Gandhi's nonviolent protest method was called "civil disobedience." This method has been studied and used by many leaders in the fights for civil rights. Martin Luther King, Jr., was a famous leader who followed Gandhi's teachings.

In 1893, Gandhi joined an Indian law firm in South Africa. Soon he was using nonviolent protests to fight discrimination. He returned to India in 1914. There Gandhi led the fight for independence from England.

Gandhi also fought discrimination by Hindus against Moslems. The Moslems were a minority in India. He worked to improve the status of the "untouchables." They were the lowest caste, or class, in India. Untouchables suffered greatly from discrimination.

Gandhi was killed in 1948, just one year after India won its independence.

traders. They were sold to plantation owners in the southern states. By ending slavery, the United States ended a part of discrimination, too. The former slaves became African Americans.

19

Ku Klux Klan members march in Houston, Texas, under police protection.

But ending slavery was just one step on the way to ending racial discrimination. After the war, some states set up special rules. These rules made it impossible for African Americans to vote or to travel without permission.

To stop these new rules, new amendments to the Constitution were passed. The 15th Amendment was one of them. This amendment gave African Americans the right to vote. African Americans were elected to many offices. Some were elected to Congress. That success made some whites angry.

The new amendments made it illegal to discriminate against African Americans. Angry whites found a new way to show their prejudice. They formed secret groups, such as the Ku

Klux Klan. They tried to frighten African Americans, and to keep them from voting. The groups did not like Catholics, Jews, or people from foreign countries. They often bullied members of these minorities. Many ugly things happened, including violence and murder. Some of the hate groups still exist today.

Since the Civil War, part of the fight against discrimination in America has taken place in the Supreme Court in Washington, D.C. It is the most powerful court in the United States. A decision by the Supreme Court affects every state and concerns every citizen.

The Supreme Court has made many decisions on cases about discrimination. A new case has often resulted in a decision overturning a law that was made before. That means a new law replaces an old one. In 1892, the Supreme Court ruled that blacks could be forced to sit in separate train cars from whites. The court said that as long as the cars were the same, segregation was legal.

But in 1954, the court tried a similar but different case. They decided that "separate but equal" was not fair. They ruled that segregation in schools was not legal, even if the schools were exactly equal. This was a very important decision. If "separate but equal" was not legal for schools, it was not legal for anything.

The year after that, an African American
woman named Rosa Parks made history. On
her way home from work in Montgomery,
Alabama, she sat in the front section of the bus.
Only white people were supposed to sit there.
She was told to move. She refused, and she
was arrested. Her arrest led to the Montgomery
Bus Boycott. African Americans refused to ride
buses until they could sit where they pleased.

That was the beginning of the American civil
rights movement in the 1950s. The movement
achieved great things. Congress passed the
Civil Rights Act in 1964, ten years after Rosa
Parks refused to move to the back of the bus.
Segregation in restaurants, parks, hotels and
other places was made illegal. One more type
of discrimination was ended.

But discrimination against African Americans
was not the only issue. While African Americans were fighting for freedom, women were
fighting too. They were seeking equality.
Women did not suffer the cruelty of slavery, but
they had hardly any more rights than slaves.
They had little choice about their lives.

The focus of the women's fight was the right
to vote. Women also fought for better pay and
the right to own property. But the fight was
long and slow. It was not until 1899 that any
women won the right to vote. And only one
state allowed that, Wyoming. Another 21 years

Leaders in the Fight Against Discrimination

Martin Luther King, Jr.

The Reverend Doctor Martin Luther King, Jr., is the best-known civil rights leader in American history. He was born in 1929. King studied the philosophy of Gandhi. He saw that nonviolence could be an important tool in the fight for civil rights. In 1955, King became famous as the leader of the Montgomery Bus Boycott.

In the following years, King led marches and demonstrations. He traveled widely, making stirring speeches. Martin Luther King, Jr. called for an end to discrimination in the United States. He was harassed, threatened, and often arrested. But the cause of civil rights in America attracted international attention under Dr. King's leadership. And the American civil rights movement inspired victims of discrimination around the world to action.

In 1964, King won the Nobel Peace Prize. Four years later, he was killed. In 1983, his birthday—January 15—was declared a national holiday in the United States.

passed before women in every state were allowed to vote.

Women and African Americans have fought against discrimination. They have won many of their battles. Their success has inspired other groups. The physically handicapped, American Indians, Hispanics, Asians, and many other groups are now fighting too.

23

In a democracy, people are free to worship as they wish.

Chapter 3

Religious and Ethnic Discrimination

Throughout history, discrimination on the basis of religion has been common. In ancient Rome, Christians faced harsh discrimination. Later, Christians split up into different groups. Even today, these groups continue to discriminate against one another. The conflict between the English and Irish Protestants and the Irish Catholics is a clear example of this. Both Catholics and Protestants are Christian, and yet they have shared a long history of discrimination.

Probably the best-known example of religious discrimination was the treatment of the Jews in

Nazi Germany. During the 1930s and 1940s, Jews were uprooted from their homes. Families were separated and sent to camps, where many were tortured, starved, and killed. In all of Europe, some 6 million Jews were murdered.

But Jews are not the only ones who have suffered because of their religion. The Armenians, for example, have faced discrimination for centuries. Most Armenians are Christian. They have been discriminated against by Muslim groups. These include Turks and Azerbaijanis.

Armenia is a land at the western end of Turkey. In the early part of this century there were riots in Turkey and some Armenians were killed. Later, rules were passed that made it illegal for Armenians to own guns or to serve in the army.

In 1915, almost all of the Armenians were forced to leave their homes. Some were killed in the streets by mobs. Others were killed by soldiers. Others were taken into the desert, where they were murdered or died of hunger. About 1 million Armenians lost their lives.

Many times we also hear about ethnic discrimination. A person's *ethnic identity* usually includes his or her religion. But it also refers to customs, language, characteristics, and the common history that a person shares as a member of a particular group.

Today, different ethnic groups discriminate against one another in many parts of the world.

Ethnic and religious discrimination is a serious problem in India, Eastern Europe, and the Middle East, to name just a few places.

In Iraq, for example, Saddam Hussein has organized discrimination against the Kurds and the Shiites. The members of these two groups are Muslims. But Saddam Hussein is also a Muslim. He is discriminating against the Kurds and the Shiites because they belong to different ethnic groups.

With the recent fall of communism, the country that was called Yugoslavia after World War I broke into several different countries. The different ethnic groups within these countries have been fighting for each other's land.

One group, the Serbs, have begun a process they call "ethnic cleansing." The Serbs want to "cleanse" the neighboring land of Bosnia by removing all non-Serbs. They especially want to drive out the Muslim residents.

More than 2 million people have been forced to leave their homes in the former Yugoslavia. And many thousands of people have died in the fighting. The Serbs are holding many Muslims in camps. They have also been accused of torturing and killing large numbers of Muslims. Even children have been murdered in the brutal conflict.

The stories of the Armenians and the Jews are tragic. So are the stories of the Muslims in Bosnia and the Kurds and Shiites in Iraq. And it is sad to think of slavery, racism, imprisonment, or any unjust treatment against any minority group. Sometimes it seems better to forget what happened in the past. Sometimes it seems easier to ignore the religious and ethnic discrimination still happening today.

Why Should We Remember?

It is important to remember the stories and events that are a part of history. History has a way of repeating itself. But if people understand and are made to face the pain, suffering, and loss of lives that have happened because of discrimination, there is a better chance that people will treat one another better in the future. Remember, when Adolf Hitler was making his plans to get rid of the Jews, he said: "Who remembers the Armenians?"

What happened to the Jews and the thousands of other victims of Hitler's Nazi Germany is now called "the Holocaust." Holocaust means "total destruction by fire." The terrors and horrors of the Holocaust all began with prejudice and discrimination. Hitler's view of the Jews and other minorities was not rational (sane). Yet a whole nation shared his distorted views and supported his efforts without question. Today, survivors of the Holocaust have pledged to make sure that the world does not forget what happened in the past. Their promise to themselves and their message to the world is "Never again."

The fighting between the Christians and the Muslims in
Beirut, Lebanon, has caused many hardships for the people.

Equal opportunity in housing is ensured by law.

Chapter 4

Fair Housing

The Civil Rights Act of 1964 made segregation illegal. But some forms of segregation have continued. Unfair housing is one of the areas where discrimination still occurs.

Sometimes, for example, African Americans are prevented from moving into certain neighborhoods. Real estate agents might tell them no houses or apartments are available in a particular neighborhood. In truth there may be houses available, but the agents may only show the property to white people. Occasionally, banks refuse to give minority people loans to buy a home.

Fair housing groups are fighting back. But it is sometimes hard to find out about this form of discrimination. Meet the Williams family. Listen to their story.

Everyone in the Williams family was nervous and excited. Mr. Williams had found a new job in another city. The family would be moving soon. But first the Williams family had to find a new home.

Joe Williams was 13 years old. He wasn't sure he wanted to move. He was happy that his father had found such a good job. But he would miss his friends from the neighborhood. He didn't want to leave them behind.

His mother told him not to worry too much. "With your father's new job, we will be able to have our own house with a yard. We won't have to live in an apartment," she said. Joe was still nervous and upset.

One Saturday afternoon, Joe and his family drove to their new city. They were going to look for a new home. It was a long drive. Joe noticed that his father seemed a little nervous. His mother was talking a lot, as if she were nervous also. This surprised Joe. He did not understand why his parents were scared. They *wanted* to move.

At last they arrived in the new city. Mrs. Williams looked at maps and gave Joe's father some directions. "I did a little research," she said. "This neighborhood is safe, mostly families with young children. And it has good schools. The prices of the houses are just right for us."

Agents cannot refuse to show houses or apartments to people because of their race or religion.

Joe looked out the window. There was a lot going on in the neighborhood. The streets were great for riding bicycles. He saw kids out on the sidewalks walking dogs and skateboarding. The grown-ups were washing their cars or mowing their lawns. Joe began to feel much better. He had always wanted a dog, but his folks didn't want to have one in an apartment. Maybe after they moved into a house, things would be different.

But Joe suddenly began to feel nervous again. He stared at the people on the street. None of them looked like him or his mother or father or sister. He was different from all the people in this neighborhood.

"Why aren't there any people here who look like us?" Joe asked his parents.

"Don't worry, Joe," his mother said. Then she saw a real estate office. "We'll go in and see if they have any houses for us to look at."

The family went inside and met the real estate agent. He was friendly. He asked what sort of house the Williams family was looking for. Mrs. Williams said she would like a house with three bedrooms. Sarah, Joe's sister, said she would like a yard. Joe thought about it for a minute. Then he said that he would like the house to be on a quiet street without too much traffic. That way he could ride a bike or play ball. Joe's father told the real estate agent what he thought he could afford to pay for a house.

The real estate agent nodded and took out some big notebooks. He looked at page after page after page. Joe saw that each page had a picture of a house. Joe was surprised by how many houses were in the book.

But the real estate agent closed the books after a while. "I'm sorry," he said. He shook his head. "We don't have anything that fits your needs."

Joe's father looked angry. His mother looked angry, too. "We've seen lots of ads for houses that we would like," she said.

"Sorry," the real estate agent said. "Maybe some other agent will have something in your price range."

Joe's mother took a newspaper ad from her pocket. "What about this house?" she said. "This one sounded just right for our family."

"Sorry," the agent said. "That has been sold already."

Joe's father stood up. "Come on, kids," he said. He looked very angry.

Out on the street, Joe was sure that people were looking at him. They acted as if they had never seen anyone who looked like him before. He wanted to tell his parents that people were staring at him. But his mom and dad were busy talking to each other.

The Williams family went down the street to another real estate office. The real estate agent there seemed friendly at first. Mr. and Mrs.

Williams described to her what kind of a house they were looking for. This time, the agent didn't even take out any books to look at. She listened for a while and then said, "I'm not sure this is the best neighborhood for you. You want good schools for your children and...."

Joe's mother interrupted the real estate agent. "This neighborhood has some of the best schools in the city," she said. " It also has a fine library and a lovely park nearby. I know because I've been researching the area."

The real estate agent looked embarrassed. She didn't expect Mrs. Williams to be so well-informed. When she started to say something, Joe's father stood up and said, "We're leaving."

Joe felt hurt and angry. He and his family had faced discrimination. They were being kept from living where they wanted to live, simply because they looked different.

Chapter 5

Stereotypes

A *stereotype* is an image of one group formed by another group. Often, discrimination is the result of negative stereotyping. Negative stereotyping happens when *all* the members of one group are seen as having certain bad characteristics—just because they belong to that group. These people are not judged as individual human beings. Instead, they are judged on the basis of their group identity.

In the United States, many groups have suffered because of stereotypes. Women, homosexuals, the physically disabled, as well as various ethnic groups, have been the more common victims. In

Canada, stereotypes hurt French Canadians, and native Canadian Indians and Eskimos (Innuit). In Australia, stereotypes of native Australians (aborigines) have been a source of conflict.

Stereotypes turn up in movies, television, and advertising. Think of the parts for African American men in many American movies and television shows. Often they play muggers, or drug dealers. In reality, most African American men are not law-breakers. But you might not know that from watching television or movies. Italian men frequently appear as gangsters or hoods. Native Americans are often shown as killers of white settlers. These are all stereotypes.

Stereotypes don't appear just on television or in the movies, though. They can turn up in everyday speech. Think of the jokes you sometimes hear about African Americans, or Jews, or Japanese. These are called *ethnic jokes*. They use stereotypes to make fun of people.

What happens if you use a stereotype? It is a way of ignoring a person as an individual. By using a stereotype, you just think of a person as part of a group. You never give the individual a chance. You will not know what is unique or special about a particular person.

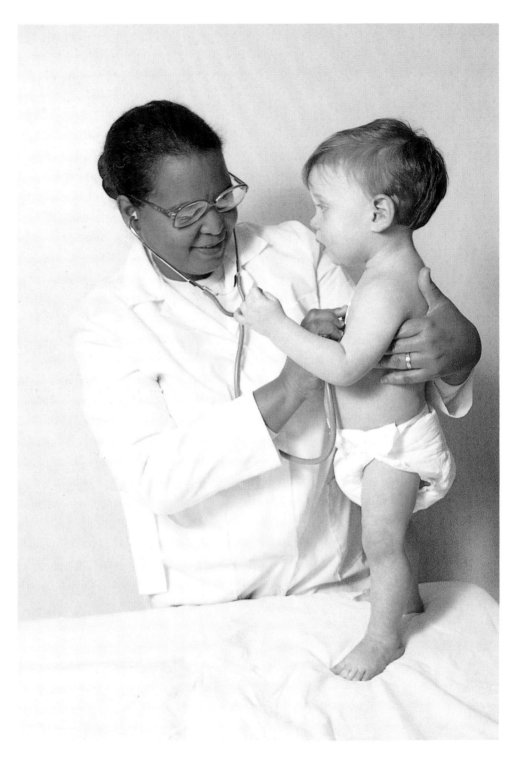

More women are entering professions that used to be reserved
for men only.

Sometimes stereotypes don't seem so bad on the surface. Sometimes they seem like compliments. You might wonder if there is anything wrong with stereotypes like that. The answer is *yes*. Let's find out why.

One stereotype of African Americans, for example, is that they are good musicians. Some people say that African Americans have "a good sense of rhythm." Another stereotype is that African Americans are good athletes.

These stereotypes seem to be positive. After all, most people wish they were great musicians or athletes. But the problem with stereotypes is beneath the surface.

It is true that African Americans as a group have given a great deal to American culture as musicians. Turn on the radio and spin the dial. Almost anything you hear has been influenced by African American composers or performers. One of America's greatest composers, Duke Ellington, was an African American.

It is also true that African Americans have been successful in sports. Think of all the great African American athletes: Hank Aaron and Willie Mays in baseball; O.J. Simpson in football; Arthur Ashe in tennis; Muhammed Ali in boxing; Kareem Abdul Jabbar in basketball; Jackie Joyner-Kersee in track.

There have been many great African American musicians and athletes. But that doesn't mean that all African Americans are good at those things. Think of how an African American who is *not* good at these things might feel. And there is a worse danger. If you believe that all African Americans are good athletes, you might not believe that they are good at other things. This kind of prejudice kept African Americans out of professions such as law and medicine for many years.

Let's look at another example of this kind of discrimination. Many people say that women are more "nurturing" than men. That means they are better at caring for, and loving, people—especially babies. Like the examples we've already seen, this stereotype seems positive. To be warm and caring is a good thing, isn't it? But if you look at this stereotype carefully, you will see a hidden meaning. The stereotype suggests that women aren't tough enough to do the jobs that men do. If they are caring, they can't be tough.

The next chapter will look at that kind of discrimination, discrimination based on sex.

It is against the law to discriminate in hiring because of sex.

Chapter 6

The Rights of Girls and Women

Girls and women have had to fight many kinds of discrimination. And much progress has been made. Girls are now able to participate and compete in activities, such as many sports, that they were excluded from in the past. More and more women are entering the work force. Many of these women have important positions and are paid high salaries.

But there is still prejudice and discrimination against women. Women are concerned about many instances where discrimination is practiced. For example, women in the work force still earn far less, overall, than men do. Working women are also concerned about affordable child care.

Women as a group express concern about their
own bodies. Many women feel that they have a
legal right to end a pregnancy (have an abortion) if
they choose. Others disagree.

One issue that women have become especially
troubled about is *sexual harassment*. Sexual harassment happens when someone makes you feel
threatened sexually by making lewd (sexually
crude) remarks, teasing, touching, asking for favors, or promising favors. It is even more of a
problem when the person who harasses a woman
is in a superior position, like a boss or a teacher.

In 1991, Clarence Thomas was nominated for
the United States Supreme Court. A committee of
senators held hearings to determine whether or
not he should be approved for the Court. During
the hearings, a law professor named Anita Hill
accused Clarence Thomas of sexual harassment.
She said the harassment had happened when they
had worked together several years before.

Eventually, Clarence Thomas was approved for
the Supreme Court. Many people did not believe
the things Anita Hill had said. But many women
felt she was very brave, and that the senators had
treated her badly. She put herself in a difficult
position. But she also made many people think
about the issue of sexual harassment.

Discrimination based on sex can happen to girls
and young women, too. Here's a story about one
girl's experience with job discrimination.

Kate James had a problem. Christmas was coming and she didn't have enough money for presents. She made a little money baby-sitting, but that was not enough. She needed a job that would pay her every week.

She talked with her parents one night after dinner. She told them why she wanted to earn money. They said that Kate could get a part-time job after school. She could also work on Saturdays.

"But you can only work three hours a day," her father said.

"That's right," said her mother. "You have to save some time for doing homework. And you need time to eat and sleep!"

Kate went to her room. Now she had to figure out what kind of work she would like to do. She had friends who worked in restaurants, but she wasn't sure she wanted that kind of job. She liked being outdoors after school, even when it was cold.

The next day she walked past the supermarket. She glanced up at the plate-glass window. It was filled with colorful signs advertising the prices of foods. One small sign caught her eye. "Delivery boy wanted," the sign said. "Must be able to work from 4 to 6 on weekdays, also Saturday mornings."

She almost jumped for joy. It was the perfect job for her. She rushed inside and asked to see the manager of the store.

The manager worked in a little office that looked out over the cash registers. He was so tall that it was hard to believe he could fit into the tiny office. But he had a friendly smile. He shook Kate's hand and gave her an application to fill out.

Once she had filled out the application, the manager asked her a few questions. He wanted to know about the classes she took, and which ones she liked best. He asked about her parents and where they lived.

Before Kate left, she told the store manager about her interest in sports. "I'm a fast runner and bike rider," she said. "I play basketball and soccer at school. I bet I could be your fastest deliverer."

The store manager laughed and shook her hand again before Kate left. "I'll call you in a day or two to let you know what I decide," he told her.

Several days passed and Kate didn't hear from him. After a week, she asked her father what to do. "Go over to the store and find out," he suggested. "Maybe the manager has been too busy to call you."

Kate hopped on her bike and rode to the store. She was about to walk in when she got a surprise. Ted Simpson, a boy in her class, was loading a box of groceries into a delivery cart. "Ted!" she said. "I didn't know you worked here."

"I just started today," he said. "I applied for the job yesterday, and today I started working."

Ted left with the cart. Kate thought about it. She had applied for the job last week. Ted applied for it yesterday. Why had *he* gotten the job?

Some employers still make decisions based on their prejudice rather than on the applicant's ability.

Women's Rights in America

1848 Seneca Falls Convention. More than a hundred men and women gathered in Seneca Falls, New York. They issued a "Declaration of Sentiments." It was similar to the Declaration of Independence. Instead of saying, "All men are created equal," it said, "All men and women are created equal."

1920 Passage of the 19th Amendment. After a long fight, women won the right to vote in every state.

1923 Equal Rights Amendment Introduced. This document said simply that there should be no discrimination on the basis of sex. It did not pass.

1965 National Organization of Women founded.

1973 Equal Rights Amendment Introduced Again. Again, after years of fighting, it did not pass. It was defeated in 1982.

Suffragettes marching

Kate went in to see the store manager. "I'm sorry I didn't call you," he said. "It just seemed the job was better suited for a boy. I'm sure you'll find some other job."

Kate wasn't so sure. The more she thought about it, the more upset she became. Ted Simpson was no bigger or stronger than she. In fact, she could probably push a cart or ride a bicycle *faster* than he could. It just wasn't fair!

On the way home, Kate looked in store and restaurant windows. No one seemed to be hiring at the moment. Now she would not have enough money for Christmas presents.

Kate's feelings were hurt. And she was angry. The store manager did not even give her a chance. He never tested her strength or speed. He thought she could not do the job just because she was a girl.

Kate had faced discrimination. Someone had judged her on the basis of her sex, not her individual ability. She felt sure she was strong enough to do the job. She had a good attitude and was willing to work hard. Now, because of discrimination, she would not get the chance to prove it.

Physically disabled people should be judged only on the basis of their ability.

Chapter 7

Sometimes It's Painful to Be Different

Discrimination can hurt people. Real estate agents did not want to sell a house to Joe's family. The family was unhappy and disappointed that they could not live where they wanted. The store manager didn't give Kate a job because she was a girl. Kate was angry and frustrated that she was not given a chance to prove herself. Kate and Joe were not judged as individuals. They were victims of discrimination.

Other Forms of Discrimination

Luis Sanchez loved to sing, and he had a very good voice. He knew how to read music. He had taken piano lessons, and he sang in his church choir.

One reason Luis worked so hard on his music was that he had a brace on his leg. He walked with a limp, and it was difficult for him to run. Luis had a physical disability. So he spent most of his time practicing his music.

Mr. Moore, the music teacher at Luis's school, announced tryouts for the school chorus. Luis was excited. He practiced very hard. And when it was his turn to sing in front of the teacher, everyone said he did a wonderful job.

Two days later the list of new chorus members was posted. Luis's name wasn't on it. When he went to ask why, Mr. Moore seemed nervous. Finally, the teacher told Luis that he could not join the chorus because of his disability.

"We have a lot of concerts where we have to move quickly on and off stage. And many times there is a long walk from the bus to the concert hall. I'm afraid it would be too difficult for you," Mr. Moore explained.

But this was not fair. Mr. Moore did not know what Luis was able to do. The teacher based his decision only on the fact that Luis had a disability.

Sometimes people are discriminated against because of their age. Some employers are prejudiced against hiring young people. Others will not consider older people for certain jobs. Discrimination because of age is illegal. But people still fight this kind of discrimination all the time, especially elderly people.

People with certain illnesses face many forms of discrimination also. Consider the story of Ryan White.

Ryan White died of AIDS in April of 1990. He was 18 years old. He had been infected with the AIDS virus when he received a blood transfusion as a young boy.

When Ryan first learned he had AIDS, he faced cruel discrimination in his hometown. Some of his classmates and their parents tried to keep him from attending school. Ryan was a victim of people's fear and lack of understanding about AIDS. Eventually, Ryan was welcomed at a school in a nearby town. But because of his experiences, Ryan White became an important spokesperson in the fight against AIDS discrimination.

Sometimes people are discriminated against because of their sexual choices. Homosexual men (gays) and homosexual women (lesbians) face this because they have partners of the same sex.

Homosexuals are thought of by many as "not normal" and "not acceptable." In recent years, gay men with AIDS in particular have faced some of the worst discrimination.

It is important to realize that discrimination in any form is hurtful and wrong. Discrimination can spread easily if it is ignored. It is only when people identify and understand the many kinds of discrimination in the world that they can become better able to fight it.

If you think you have been discriminated against, you can contact government agencies for help.

Chapter 8

Dealing with Discrimination

Even though progress was made during the civil rights movement, discrimination is still a serious problem in America. In fact, some people feel it is getting worse.

Discrimination is unjust. And more important, discrimination is dangerous.

Discrimination and Violence

In 1992, in a part of New York City called the Bronx, a young black boy and his younger sister were walking to school. Suddenly they were attacked by a group of white boys. These boys held the black children down and painted their faces with white shoe polish. They told the children, "Now you're white like us."

Fortunately, this boy and his sister were only frightened and not seriously hurt. But sometimes violence goes along with discrimination. In recent years, a number of people (blacks and whites) have been killed because of being in the "wrong neighborhood." In other words, they were killed only because of the color of their skin or their ethnic identity, not because of anything they did.

Discrimination is a serious problem in other countries, too. In 1989 and 1990, Communist governments fell in many countries in Europe. But when communism fell, many people began to form strong ties to their ethnic groups.

There have been many instances of discrimination of one ethnic group against another in these countries. In Germany, for example, angry young people known as "skinheads" have been discriminating against foreigners in their country. Much of this discrimination has been very violent.

Sometimes, the violence of discrimination can come from the *victims* of discrimination. People who have been discriminated against often feel frustration. This frustration can grow into anger as the discrimination continues. Finally, it can lead to violence.

That is what happened in Los Angeles, California, in the spring of 1992. African Americans and other minorities in Los Angeles felt that the police force there had discriminated against them for many years. In March of 1991, a group of white police officers were accused of severely beating a black man named Rodney King. But at their trial, the jury pronounced these officers not guilty. The frustration and anger of African Americans as well as other minorities in Los Angeles exploded into violence. Fighting, burning, looting, and rioting went on for several days. There were incidents of violence in several other American cities as well.

Fighting Discrimination

There are things all of us can do to stop discrimination. Like Susan B. Anthony, Mohandas K. Gandhi, Martin Luther King, Jr., and others, we must not be afraid to fight discrimination.

In some schools, people are learning new forms of *conflict resolution*. Conflict resolution programs provide students and teachers with new ways to solve problems. They learn about tolerance and how to see another point of view. They try to find a common ground when they work with people and groups who are not getting along.

Some churches, synagogues, and community-based organizations are also exploring ways to deal with discrimination. There are also national organizations that have been set up to fight discrimination in the United States. Several of these groups are listed under "Where to Get Help" at the back of this book. In addition to those listed, groups like Human Rights Watch and Amnesty International are fighting discrimination throughout the world.

If you think you have faced discrimination, tell
somebody. If you know someone who is being
discriminated against, speak up for that person.
Remember that most discrimination is illegal. If
you or your family face discrimination, there are
government agencies you may wish to contact.
Keep talking about your feelings until you find help.

Remember the stories about Joe, Kate, and Luis.
All three faced discrimination. But their stories did
not end there.

Joe's mother wrote a letter to the local newspaper about the neighborhood where her family
wanted to move. A man who was moving from the
area saw her letter. He offered to sell his house to
Joe's family.

Kate went to talk to the store manager again.
She told him she thought he had been unfair. She
showed him how strong she was by carrying several heavy boxes of groceries out of the store. He
was impressed. The manager told her he needed a
second delivery person. He offered her the job.

Two of Luis's friends told a favorite teacher what
had happened with the chorus tryouts. She was
very angry. She went to talk to Mr. Moore about it.
Mr. Moore listened to her ideas, and the next week
he said Luis could join the chorus.

You will be involved in many different situations,
at home, in school, on the job, and in social set-
tings. If you suspect that you are being treated
unfairly, take a closer look. Ask yourself honestly

why things happened the way they did. What part did you play? How much did you try to help yourself? How did you compare to others who had the same goal as you? Was the outcome based on your attitude, ability, education, or experience? Or was it based only on your age, race, sex, or religion?

You can learn to recognize discrimination and take immediate action to fight it. Even one person can make a difference. You can make things better for yourself and for others. And each person who decides to fight discrimination becomes part of the *solution* instead of part of the problem.

Glossary—*Explaining New Words*

apartheid A system of rules in South Africa that is designed to prevent the black majority from gaining control of society.

communism A one-party form of government that works primarily for the good of the state rather than the individual.

conflict resolution A system for dealing with tension between individuals or groups. Learning new ways to solve problems.

discrimination Action taken based on prejudice.

ethnic identity A person's image of himself or herself based on belonging to a particular group. The group shares a common history, customs, language, and religion.

ethnic jokes Humorous remarks that make fun of people because of their ethnic identity.

individual rights Rights that apply to each person regardless of race, religion, age, or sex.

majority The largest group in society.

minority One of many smaller groups in society.

physical disability (handicap) A condition one is born with or that results from an illness or injury, making some activities more difficult. A disabled person may be blind, deaf, lame, or paralyzed.

prejudice Hatred of a particular group, race, or religion that has no basis in fact.

segregation Separation of people by races. In the United States, segregation is illegal.

sexual harassment Any unwanted or inappropriate sexual attention, including touching, looks, comments, or gestures.

stereotype A belief that all members of a certain group act in the same way or believe in the same things. Lack of regard for members of the group as individuals.

tolerance Freedom from prejudice; willingness to listen and treat others with respect in spite of any differences.

Where To Get Help

Office of the General Counsel
United States Commission on Civil Rights
1121 Vermont Avenue NW
Washington, D.C. 20425

Southern Law Poverty Center
Klanwatch Project
400 Washington Avenue, P.O. Box 548
Montgomery, AL 36195-5101

Anti-Defamation League of B'nai Brith
Offices nationwide; check your phone book or
the phone book for the city nearest your town.

Urban League
Offices nationwide; check your phone book or
the phone book for the city nearest your town.

NAACP (National Association for the Advance-
  ment of Colored People)
4805 Mt. Hope Drive
Baltimore, MD 21215

If you need legal help, contact your local Public Defender's Office, Legal Aid Society, Legal Assistance Association, or state chapter of the American Civil Liberties Union.

For Further Reading

Edwards, Gabrielle I. *Coping with Discrimination*, rev. ed. New York: Rosen Publishing Group, 1992. This book talks about discrimination in its many forms, and what you can do about it.

Manetti, Lisa. *Equality*. New York: Franklin Watts, 1989. A history of civil rights in the United States.

Osborn, Kevin. *Tolerance*, rev. ed. New York: Rosen Publishing Group, 1993. Explains why tolerance is the foundation of peace.

Wartski, Maureen Crane. *A Long Way from Home*. Philadelphia: The Westminster Press, 1980. A young Vietnamese refugee struggles to find a place for himself in an often inhospitable America.

Wharton, Mandy. *Rights of Women*. New York: Glouchester Press, 1989. The story of the fight for women's rights around the world.

Index

63

About the Author
Ezra Palmer is a journalist and writer. He lives in New York with his wife and family.

About the Editor
Evan Stark is a well-known sociologist, educator, and therapist as well as a popular lecturer on women's rights and children's health issues. He is the author of many publications in the field of family relations and is the father of four children.

Acknowledgments and Photo Credits
Cover: Blackbirch Graphics, Inc.; pp. 10, 48: Culver Pictures, Inc.; p. 11: The Associated Press; p. 15: Library of Congress; p. 16: Bettmann Archive; p. 17: Stuart Rabinowitz; pp. 19, 23, 29: Wide World Photos, Inc.; p. 20: Bettmann Newsphotos. All other photographs by Barbara Kirk.

Design/Production: Blackbirch Graphics, Inc.